LISBON TRAVEL GU

"Exploring Lisbon: Insider Insights for 2024 Adventurers

MELISSA KELLUM

Table of Contents

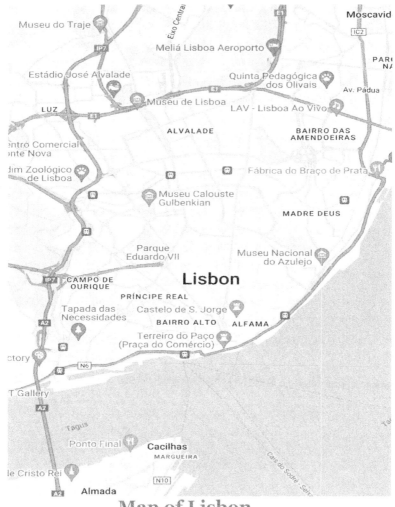

Map of Lisbon

Your travel schedule

INTRODUCTION

Put an end to the planned itineraries and
sterilised scenery. This isn't just a trip guide
for sun worshippers and history buffs
crossing out sites for pictures. This is an
invitation to a mysterious city where
shadows dance around sun-drenched
squares and mysteries murmur from ancient
corridors. Lisbon is calling the curious, the
daring, and those who seek the excitement
of the unknown with great attraction.

Picture the fragrance of grilled sardines and
cappuccino mingling with the scent of a salt-
kissed air. The cobblestones under your feet
are a silent testament to the vibrant and
sometimes violent history of this city. They

have been worn smooth by centuries of foot traffic. Hear the echoes of ancient stories echoing through Alfama's winding lanes, the melancholy strains of fado clinging to the damp stones like ghosts of dreams long gone.

Lisbon is a puzzle that has to be solved rather than a city to be taken over. Its allure lies not in the usual postcard pretty, but in the intricate web of historical details, hushed tales, and vibrant contradictions that weave together to create its unique fabric. In this city, opulent basilicas coexist side by side with crumbling ruins, each telling tales of vanished empires and unsaid whispers.

Ascend the rickety Tram 28 and use it to serve as your transport across time. Navigate the narrow streets of Alfama, where houses with ochre hues cling awkwardly to one another and secrets protrude from balconies adorned with crimson flowers. Fado is a melancholic song about love lost, longing, and the resilient spirit of a city that has weathered literal and metaphorical storms. Let its melancholic sounds wash over you.

However, Lisbon is more than just a place of doleful whispers. The city is alive with energy, with sunny days giving way to lively nights brimming with Bairro Alto's joyful chaos. Laughter bursts from open windows here, mingling with the sound of glasses clinking and the irresistible beat of salsa spilling into the cobblestone streets. The avant-garde and industrial warehouse ghosts coexist at the vibrant LX Factory, where bold paintings adorn the walls and the buzz of artistic activity fills the air.

And when the noise of the city becomes too much, escape to the serene serenity of Jerónimos Monastery. Allow its magnificent carvings to tell tales of swift triumphs and whispers of a bygone era. Alternatively, lose yourself in the verdant haven of Ajuda Botanical Garden, where rare flowers bloom under the watchful shadow of ancient trees.

Lisbon is a city that embraces its contradictions; it's a patchwork of modern beats and antiquated murmurs, grand avenues and unmarked alleys, sun-kissed illusions and whispered secrets. It's a city that hides its true nature well, demanding an inquisitive mind, an adventurous spirit, and an openness to the unexpected.

This is not a manual for the timid among us. This song is alluring for individuals who like the bittersweet taste of the unknown, are adventurers, and are looking for lost treasures. Lisbon is calling you to go into the shadows, explore the mysteries, and dance with the fancies of sun-kissed dreams it stores inside its palm.

Are you prepared? Flip the page and let Lisbon's melody to envelop you.

CHAPTER ONE

About Lisbon

Lisbon is a city you fall into, not one you visit. Not with a thump, but rather with a leisurely, entrancing descent into midnight alleys and sun-drenched squares, where generations whisper their tales in the murmur of fado's heartfelt sorrow. This is a love letter to Lisbon's wild essence, a symphony of secrets performed on cobblestones worn smooth by years of laughing and desire. Forget polished landscapes and planned itineraries.

Shut your eyes. Inhale the scent of grilled sardines and espresso combined with the briny kiss of the Atlantic. Feel the beat of the city under your feet, a rhythm made of the loud laughter resonating from secret tabernas, the melancholy screams of seabirds, and the banging of trams. Through the winding lanes of Alfama, hear the murmurs of a thousand stories. Sun-bleached buildings bend in closeness, their antique walls embellished with half-truths and secrets just waiting to be exposed.

Lisbon is a tapestry, not a place to visit. Richly decorated with baroque flourishes and Moorish arches, the city has seen the rise and fall of many civilizations, as shown by the decaying remains next to glittering basilicas. Here, the sun creates multicolored shadows that dance with the ghosts of old laughter, painting brief fantasies on fading Azulejo tiles.

Board Tram 28, your flimsy time-traveling carriage. Navigate the winding streets of Alfama, where homes with ochre hues murmur secrets like conspirators and balconies reveal secrets like petals wafting in the air. Allow the fado to envelop you, a melancholic symphony that conveys the essence of saudade, a profound yearning for the past, and an abiding affection for the city that holds your heart. The past is more than just a memory in these dimly lit alleyways; it's a live presence that inhales the aroma of grilled sardines and pulses with the beat of flamenco dancing.

Lisbon, nevertheless, is more than simply a city of gloomy rumors. The city is alive with energy, with sunny days giving way to colorful evenings brimming with Bairro Alto's exuberant mayhem. Here, the sound of salsa spilling into the cobblestone streets, mixed with the clinking of drinks and laughing coming from open windows. The avant-garde and industrial warehouse ghosts coexist at LX Factory, where the walls are covered in bold murals and resounding with the sound of artistic activity.

And retreat to Jerónimos Monastery's subdued tranquility when the city's clamor fades to a whisper. Allow its elaborate carvings to evoke memories of a golden past and legends of naval triumphs. Alternatively, let yourself disappear inside the lush Ajuda Botanical Garden, where exotic flowers blossom under the watchful shadow of ancient trees, each leaf serving as a reminder of life's tenacity—much like Lisbon itself.

Lisbon is a city that embraces its opposites; it's a kaleidoscope of contemporary rhythms and evocative whispers, wide avenues and hidden passageways, sun-kissed fantasies and whispered secrets. It's a city that demands curiosity, a desire for adventure, and an openness to the unexpected; it doesn't disclose itself readily.

This is not a manual for the timid among you. This is an invitation to dance with the sun-kissed fantasies Lisbon holds in its hand, go into the darkness, and solve the mysteries. Allow the aroma of seared sardines to mislead you. Embrace the laughter that seeps out of secret tabernas. Follow the fado echoes along meandering alleys. Your own hidden tale is waiting for you inside Lisbon's tapestry.

Flip the page and let the song of Lisbon carry you away. You'll be a part of Lisbon's colorful, entrancing symphony—a tune played on cobblestones and murmured in shadows, a song of sun-kissed fantasies and saudade's tender sorrow—rather than simply a tourist.

Geography of Lisbon

Lisbon is a geographical marvel, not simply a city. Picture the spot where the Tagus River, a ribbon of glistening silver, gently embraces a metropolis as it kisses the Atlantic Ocean. Here, gently sloping hills give way to the lake; terracotta roofs and historic fortifications adorn their summits. Lisbon is a symphony of water and stone, where the landscape creates a mesmerizing tune of its own.

- A City Sculpted by Rivers:

Lisbon's vitality is derived from the Tagus River, which flows through the center of the city. It shapes the terrain, chiseling away at the cobblestones of Alfama and chiseling out magnificent cliffs. For millennia, its seas have seen the rise and fall of empires, the setting forth of explorers, and the casting of nets by fisherman. Ride a boat across its glistening surface and see the city opening out in front of you like a historical map.

- Hills that Recount History:

Lisbon is a city with history etched into its very hills; it is not a level place. Like emerald gems, seven hills rise, each with a distinctive crown. Tales of Moorish origins abound in Alfama, which clings to the easternmost hill, while Castelo, capped by São Jorge Castle, speaks of a magnificent history as a fortified bastion. Ascend Graça hill to the Miradouro da Senhora do Monte, where you will be met with an astounding panoramic view of far-off hills melting into the distance, glistening water, and red houses.

- Where Ocean Meets City:

Lisbon's heart moves in time with the waves. With a hint of sea salt, the Atlantic air whispers secrets in your ear. Imagine the hopes of navigators carved into the very stones as you stroll down the Ribeira das Naus, the site where formerly caravels set sail for unexplored seas. The immensity of the ocean stretched out in front of you at Belém Tower, a sentinel watching over the entrance of the Tagus, inviting you to go on an adventure.

- Beyond the Urban Embrace:

Lisbon's topography, however, extends beyond its boundaries. When you get beyond the urban sprawl, you'll find lush hills covered with olive and grape groves.

Take a hike through the expansive Monsanto Forest Park, which carries whispers of secret passageways and long-forgotten mysteries. Unwind on Guincho Beach's golden beaches while the waves lap against the coast like far-off drums.

Lisbon's topography is a narrative expressed via wind, water, and stone. The canvas is adorned with undulating hills, glistening rivers, and the boundless ocean. The tune beckons you to meander, investigate, and immerse yourself in the tales etched into the city's own foundations and the mysteries murmured by the sea. Come, embrace the topography of Lisbon, and explore the beauty entwined with every turn and twist.

History and culture

Lisbon is not a city of museums, stuck in the past in muted tones. It's a living tapestry fashioned from centuries of legends, in which Roman legionaries and Phoenician tradesmen shook hands, Moorish artists left their elaborate flourishes, and daring adventurers dreamed of undiscovered lands. Lisbon is a city where history hums its own passionate symphony, the cobblestones echoing with the thrum of saudade, a painful desire for the past, and the whispers of empires.

- Echoes of Empires:

Explore Alfama, a winding labyrinth of ochre-hued cottages and tiny passageways, and you'll sense the lingering echoes of Moorish influence in the atmosphere. Look up to São Jorge Castle, a solemn reminder of Portugal's might in the Middle Ages, a stoic sentinel standing atop the tallest hill. Admire the exquisite Manueline sculptures at the Jerónimos Monastery, which pay homage to nautical triumphs and speak of a bygone era when Portuguese ships traveled the world.

- From Caravels to Cobblestones:

Lisbon's history is woven into the very fabric of the city, not only carved onto stone. When caravels once opened their sails, carrying hopes of other planets, you might stand at Belém Tower. Imagine Ferdinand Magellan embarking on his journey, or Vasco da Gama plotting his route to India, their spirits still lingering in the ocean wind. Once a thriving harbor neighborhood, Belém has cobblestone lanes. Follow them to experience a bygone era of adventure and ambition.

- Extraordinary Monuments:

Yet Lisbon's spirit isn't limited to its imposing structures. Explore the bustling Bairro Alto, where the sad strains of fado waft out of secret tabernas, each note telling a narrative of love lost and the gentle anguish of saudade. Explore the renovated industrial facilities of LX Factory, which are teeming with inventive spirit and creative energy. Discover the vibrant Campo de Ourique markets, where artisanal goods and fresh vegetables from generations-old merchants will entice you to explore.

- A Melting Pot of Cultures:

Lisbon has long been a city at a crossroads, where customs and cultures have blended together. Ancient cathedrals are decorated with Moorish tiles, Bairro Alto is alive with African rhythms, and the contagious joie de vivre of the city is infused with Brazilian influences. Lisbon's cultural tapestry, a symbol of its openness and tenacity, is its beating heart.

- Fado: Saudade's Song:

Lisbon is more than simply its districts and monuments; its spirit may be heard in the melancholic melodies of fado. Originating in the backstreets of Alfama, this heartbreaking song tells of love, grief, and saudade—a profound yearning for the past while still fervently embracing the present. Take in the fado's tune as it floats through your mind, a melancholy but lively, resilient yet nostalgic reflection of Lisbon's character.

- A City that Embraces Today:

Lisbon, however, is not mired in the past. This metropolis pulsates with a young vitality and an unquenchable yearning for the new, dancing to the beat of the modern day. See the creative energy blooming in disused warehouses at LX Factory, where colorful street art adorns previously unnoticed alleyways. Chic cafés mix with vintage bookshops in Chiado, while creative eateries play with regional cuisine.

Lisbon boldly displays its past, much like a well-worn robe embellished with glistening strands of the present. It's a city where the melancholy tune of fado sings odes to saudade and whispers tales from old cobblestones. Discover the city's lively energy, accept its paradoxes, and immerse yourself in the history, culture, and constantly changing future of this ever-changing metropolis. Come stroll the streets of Lisbon, relish its distinct charm, and let its music to enchant you.

CHAPTER TWO

Planning your trip

Arranging a vacation to Lisbon is like setting off on a tour through a rich tapestry of culture, history, and natural beauty. Portugal's capital city, which is tucked away along the Tagus River, entices visitors with a seductive fusion of contemporary beauty and old-world elegance, guaranteeing an unforgettable encounter that will live long in the mind.

The excitement of discovering Lisbon's complex personality—a city with cobblestone lanes that connect to old areas and historical sites that tower above modern life—is at the heart of organizing this adventure. Initiating this voyage requires delving into the wealth of opportunities

Lisbon offers and painstakingly crafting a schedule that encapsulates its spirit.

Situated atop one of Lisbon's seven hills, the São Jorge Castle offers panoramic views that effortlessly merge antiquity with the city's contemporary sprawl, illustrating the city's rich past. The oldest neighborhood in Lisbon, Alfama, entices visitors to get lost in its winding lanes and discover hidden treasures and local hangouts that characterize the true essence of Lisbon. The neighborhood is known for its pastel-colored buildings and winding passageways. Furthermore, Lisbon's vibrant cultural scene adds even more appeal to the journey. In private pubs, the alluring beat of Portugal's lyrical Fado music genre fills the air with stories of romance and desire. Lisbon's artistic essence is waiting to be discovered around every corner, as shown by the colorful street art that covers buildings all throughout the city.

There are many options available when choosing a place to stay in Lisbon, ranging from luxurious boutique hotels with views of the Tagus River to quaint guesthouses hidden away in old areas. Every choice offers a different viewpoint on the city, enabling visitors to really experience Lisbon's allure.

The foundation of every trip to Lisbon is culinary discovery. The scent of freshly made Pastéis de Nata, the well-known custard tarts from Portugal, fills the air and entices the senses to explore the culinary wonders of the city. Lisbon's food scene is a feast for the senses, with everything from delicious seafood at Mercado da Ribeira to traditional Portuguese fare at family-run restaurants.

Traveling beyond the city boundaries reveals riches that are waiting to be found. Day visits to Lisbon's neighboring attractive seaside town of Cascais or the enchanted town of Sintra, with its lush gardens and opulent palaces, provide a break from the city's bustle and a glimpse of Portugal's varied landscapes.

Organizing logistics is just one aspect of the art of trip planning to Lisbon; the other is living up to the expectation of an experience that goes beyond sightseeing. It's about letting oneself get carried away by the city's attractiveness, becoming involved with its residents, and embracing its beat.

Lisbon's magnetic draw is undeniable as the schedule takes form and the excitement mounts, guaranteeing an experience that will beyond expectations and leave the visitor with priceless memories. Carefully thought out to the last detail, the trip to Lisbon is a symphony of expectation, with each moment meant to be treasured in the mosaic of travel encounters.

Best time to visit

Lisbon is not a city that exists just in calendars. It's a symphony of whispers from the seaside and sun-kissed streets, with a rhythm that changes with the seasons and reveals a different song for the inquisitive mind with every chapter. So set aside travel guides and weather apps, and let your emotions serve as a compass as we discover

Lisbon's captivating enchantment as seen through the prism of time.

- Spring's Blush: A City in Blossom:

Lisbon wakes up with a flush as the last of the winter's cold fades. Terracotta buildings are painted in vivid colors by the crimson bougainvillea that cascades down balconies. Orange blossom fragrance permeates the air, while jacaranda trees drape cobblestone pathways in dreamy purple canopies. The days get longer, beckoning leisurely lunches in squares bathed in sunlight and walks by the Tagus, whose surface glitters like a ribbon of sapphire. Cafés overflow onto pavements, the sound of laughing blending with the steady clinking of glasses. Lisbon is waltzing into life in the springtime, brimming with young exuberance and an infectious joie de vivre.

- Summer's Sizzle: Sun-Kissed Dreams and Salty Secrets:

As the sun rises higher, Lisbon becomes a golden light playground. The alluring sound of warm sand and turquoise oceans is what draws people to beaches. While Cascais depicts an image of sophisticated beachfront appeal, Guincho Beach whispers stories of surfers surfing the wind-kissed waves. The cheerful pandemonium of sardinha festivals fills the air in the historic center, accompanied by the smokey fragrance of grilled delights and the sound of clinking glasses and laughing. Evenings dissolve into colorful murals of music and street acts, Bairro Alto pulsating with the contagious rhythm of salsa and the melancholic lament of fado resonating from obscure tabernas. The summer months in Lisbon are a kaleidoscope of saline secrets and sun-kissed fantasies, a time to immerse oneself in the captivating pulse of the city.

- Autumn's Tapestry: Melancholy Melodies and Tranquil Whispers:

Lisbon welcomes a new tune when the sun sets and the leaves put on their golden cloaks. The city shrouds itself in an ethereal splendor, with alleys and squares enveloped in a golden silence. The perfume of freshly brewed espresso and fallen leaves tinges the air, beckoning small talk in quaint cafés. The days are filled with peaceful expeditions, secret courtyards that reveal riches glistening with gold, and museums that murmur historical stories. The detailed sculptures at Jerónimos Monastery appear to become more tragic in the subdued light, as their tales seem to delve deeper into gloom. Introspection, soaking up the calmer side of Lisbon, and listening to the mournful tune of fado as it paints paintings of saudade on the canvas of dusk are all encouraged during the autumn season in Lisbon.

- Winter's Embrace: Cozy Corners and Festive Firelight:

Lisbon curls into a warm embrace as the wind whispers stories of other places and the Tagus becomes a steely gray. Christmas lights turn the city into a fantasy straight out of a fairy tale, twinkling over squares like falling stars. The air is filled with the smells of roasted chestnuts and cinnamon, drawing you into cozy tabernas where the deeper resonance of Fado's sorrowful cry can be heard. Lisbon's winter months are perfect for cozy fireside conversations, substantial stews enjoyed in candlelight dining establishments, and museum exploration of hidden gems like the Museu Nacional do Azulejo, whose colorful tile walls whisper tales of warmth and heritage.

Therefore, don't inquire when to visit Lisbon, oh tourist. Find the tune that speaks to your spirit. Do you long for the blush of spring blossoms, the sun-kissed joy of summer, the quiet beauty of autumn, or the coziness of winter? In Lisbon, each season is a distinct chapter, a melody just waiting to be heard. Come explore the heart of Lisbon, let its beat lead you, and be enchanted by the charm that emerges in each season. Lisbon is a city that moves to its own unique, year-round pulse.

Budgeting tips

Lisbon, the sun-drenched city where fado paints sunsets with saudade and cobblestones whisper tales, doesn't have to break the budget. Explore this dynamic combination of contemporary activity and antique beauty—even if your vacation budget is more on the "shoestring." So forget expensive excursions and fancy brochures; we're going to show you how to navigate Lisbon on a shoestring, making tasty sardines your feast and cobblestone alleyways your playground.

- Accommodation Aficionado:

Intimates become into allies rather than merely somewhere to stay. Lisbon has a thriving hostel industry that offers accommodations for social butterflies and all sleeping preferences. Visit the Social Hostel Lisboa, where hammocks and a courtyard promise bohemian happiness, or We Love Fado Hostel in Alfama, which has a distinctive appeal and a rooftop patio. If sharing an Airbnb with your traveling companions is more your style, you may even be able to get a rooftop with captivating city views.

- Foodie Fun on the Fly:

The Mercado do Ribeira is where your gastronomic journey begins; forget upscale dining establishments. Fresh fruit, delicious pastries, and enough gourmet sandwiches to last all day are available in this busy paradise of local pleasures. Bonus: pack a picnic and go visit Jardim do Estrela, the romantic secret-sputtering fountains with strutting peacocks. Go to Belem and its waterfront eateries for affordable seafood; steamy bowls of caldeirada (fish stew) and grilled sardines will satisfy your inner foodie without breaking the wallet.

- Free-Spirited Explorations:

Lisbon is a free-loving city, therefore you should be too! Give up on the costly excursions and trust in your own strength. Get lost in Alfama's winding streets, where there are secret azulejo tiles and sun-drenched patios around every turn. For the purchase of a decent pair of walking shoes, climb to Miradouro da Senhora do Monte for breathtaking panoramic views. Take Tram 28 for the nostalgic experience of rattling past quaint neighborhoods and seeing residents going about their daily lives, rather than for the fastest journey.

- Cultural Curiosities on a Dime:

Museums are open to the public! On some days, usually in conjunction with special events or exhibits, many provide free admission. Take advantage of the free Sundays at the Museu Nacional de Arte Antiga and the Thursdays at the Museu Nacional do Azulejo. Every Saturday afternoon, the Museu Coleção Berardo, which has an amazing collection of modern masterpieces, is free for fans of modern art. Bonus advice: bring a picnic lunch and eat it in the peaceful courtyard of the museum.

- Transportation Triumphs:

Step by step, by step, by step! Lisbon is a small city that is best seen on foot. Discover undiscovered gems, experience the authentic atmosphere, and save your euros for a rich pastel de nata (custard tart). Take the metro when your feet need a rest; it's economical, efficient, and gives you an opportunity to meet locals. The 7 Colinas card is ideal for a day of neighborhood exploration as it provides unrestricted travel on public transportation for a whole day. If you have to go further, think about taking the boat over the Tagus River, which provides breathtaking vistas and an affordable excitement.

- Hidden Gems and Handy Hacks:

Lisbon loves rewarding inquisitive people. Look for free cultural activities and festivals all year long, including as outdoor cinema screenings at São Jorge Castle and jazz concerts in Chiado. For free local knowledge and insider recommendations, take a walking tour. Bring a reusable bottle of water; Lisbon has plenty of drinking fountains to keep you hydrated and your pocketbook pleased. Haggling is part of the excitement of flea markets, so don't be scared to haggle! Lastly, enjoy the siesta by taking a leisurely lunch break around noon and avoiding expensive tourist traps at busy times.

- The Lisbon Budget Mantra:

Remember, fine dining establishments and five-star hotels aren't where Lisbon's enchantment lies. It's in the sound of sun-drenched laughter resonating across plazas, the clinking of glasses in secret bodegas, and the salty spray of the Tagus River on your face.

Transportation guide

For the unfamiliar, Lisbon—a city where historic cobblestones entwine with contemporary avenues—can seem like a maze. It may appear difficult to navigate its hills, busy squares, and quaint lanes, but fear not, wanderlust-stricken wanderer! This book will act as your chauffeur, guiding you through the varied array of transportation alternatives Lisbon has to offer and making sure you don't miss a single secret or picturesque view.

- Metro: The Quick Subterranean Snake:

The sleek, silver Lisbon Metro, affectionately known as "o metro," is your ride through the center of the city. Underneath the cityscape are four linked, color-coded lines that provide quick links between important locations. A rechargeable Viva Viagem card unlocks the greatest rates on tickets, and you may hop on and off trams, buses, and even ferries.

Tickets are reasonably priced. Expert advice: To avoid penalties, validate your ticket at the yellow machines before accessing the station.

- Trains: Time-Traveling Enchantresses:

Experience a nostalgic trip through time on one of Lisbon's famous trams. Tram 28, the traditional yellow carriage, rustles between Graça and Alfama, providing picturesque views of sun-dappled squares and terracotta houses. Other tram lines, such as the elétrico 24E, wind past Jerónimos Monastery and Belém Tower as they pass through the heart of medieval Belém. Keep in mind that these beauties might become crowded, so you'll need patience and a sense of humor.

- Buses: Threading Through Residential Areas:

The vast bus network covers the whole city, getting to places the metro doesn't. Take a bus trip along the Tagus River to enjoy the scenery, or walk through the tiny alleys of Alfama, which are too small for trams. In general, buses are reasonably priced, and the Viva Viagem card is accepted here. Get the Citymapper app to stay on top of bus schedules and routes in real time, so you never get lost in the labyrinth.

- Ferries: A Bit of Exploration:

Lisbon is proud of its waterfront, and taking the boat gives you a different viewpoint. Sail across the Tagus River, taking in the picturesque view of the city skyline. Alight at Cacilhas to indulge in delectable seafood and quaint cafés. Take a longer trip and take the boat to Trafaria, a quaint fishing hamlet where it feels like time has stopped. Expert advice: Take a picnic and watch the breathtaking sunset from your terrace.

- Funiculars and Elevators: Overcoming the Hills:

Lisbon's terrain is far from level, thus navigating its slopes becomes a challenge in and of itself. With its ironwork wonder that evokes the Eiffel Tower, the Santa Justa Lift transports you to the charming Chiado neighborhood and its beautiful vistas. Bairro Alto's funicular train, the Ascensor da Glória, makes for a lovely ascent that unveils beautiful villas perched on hillsides and secret patios.

- Ridesharing and Taxis: When Velocity Is Essential:

Taxis and ridesharing applications such as Bolt and Uber are easily accessible for those who are in a rush. Taxis are metered, and it's normal to hail one while driving. Before embarking on your trip, don't forget to verify the fare shown on the screen. Particularly for shared journeys, ridesharing applications are convenient and often have affordable costs.

- Walking: Discovering Undiscovered Treasures:

Walking is the greatest way to enjoy Lisbon to the fullest. Put on your walking shoes, explore Alfama's winding alleyways, discover secret plazas with azulejos tiles, and take in the atmosphere of the area. For panoramic views, climb to Miradouro da Senhora do Monte. Alternatively, visit Bairro Alto's hip stores and lively cafés.

Keep in mind that discovering the city's hidden gems is often best accomplished by getting lost.

- Cyclists: Two Wheels, Infinite Options:

Take a bike and ride around the city's network of cycling trails if you're feeling daring. Lisbon has developed a growing bike-friendly infrastructure, with bike lanes and rental stores dotted across the city. Take a leisurely stroll along the riverbank promenade, go cycling on the Tagus, or visit the Monsanto Forest Park to get some fresh air. For a safe and fun ride, just don't forget to wear a helmet and abide by traffic laws.

Outside the City Boundaries:

The doorway to more of Portugal's treasures is Lisbon. Trains carry you to Cascais, a little coastal resort with golden beaches and mouthwatering cuisine, or Sintra, a fantasy town tucked away in the hills. For a smooth travel experience, think about taking a day trip to these locations using the integrated Viva Viagem card.

- Transportation Advice for a Comfortable Journey:
- ✓ To get about Lisbon affordably and conveniently, buy a Viva Viagem card.
- ✓ Before entering the metro station, validate your ticket at the yellow machines.
- ✓ When using public transportation, pay attention to peak hours, particularly during rush hours.
- ✓ Get the Citymapper app to get the most recent bus schedules and routes.

✓ For discovering undiscovered treasures and taking in the local flavor, think about strolling.

CHAPTER THREE

Exploring neighbourhood

Lisbon, the sun-drenched city entwined with contemporary rhythms and eons-old murmurs, cries out to be discovered beyond the glossy travel brochures and set routes. Its many neighborhoods, each a tapestry of history, culture, and distinct appeal, are its throbbing heart. Let curiosity be your guide as we explore the colorful tapestry of Lisbon's districts, which is just waiting to be discovered. So throw away your maps and guidebooks, dear visitor.

- Alfama: The Soul of Fado and Azulejos, Where Time Whispers:

Start your adventure at Alfama, the historic heart of Lisbon. Get lost in its winding alleyways, where buildings with ochre hues lean intimately, their walls covered with vivid azulejos tiles that mutter tales of Moorish ancestry. A secret patio, a sunlit plaza, or a modest bodega where the sad strains of fado seep into the cobblestones, painting images of saudade on the canvas of dusk, are revealed around every turn. Scale the tallest hill to reach the Castelo de São Jorge, a stoic sentinel that will leave a lasting impression on your mind. The past is alive and well in Alfama, where it can be heard resonating from doors, sardines frying in the fragrance, and flamenco feet pounding on sun-warmed stones.

- Bairro Alto: A Place Where Laughter Pours Out of Windows and Bohemian Beats Pulsate:

Enter Bairro Alto's throbbing energy from Alfama's murmurs. This lively area is a canvas covered in graffiti, with its winding lanes full of independent shops, hip cafés, and treasures just waiting to be found. Bairro Alto comes alive as the sky is painted in flaming colors at twilight. A combination of the heartfelt lament of fado, the exhilarating pounding of salsa, and the clinking of glasses in warm tabernas flows out of open windows. Take in the infectious laughter of the people as you meander through the labyrinth of alleys and stumble across spontaneous music gatherings in obscure places. The nighttime in Bairro Alto beckons you to immerse yourself in the lively pulse of the city, whispering secrets of inventiveness and unbridled delight.

- Chiado: The Coffee Shop Where Hipsters and History Meet:

Then enter Chiado's graceful embrace. This delightful combination of old and contemporary is still present in this historic quarter, which was previously frequented by literary giants and bohemian artists. Elegant cafés with elaborate exteriors invite you in for a leisurely croissant and coffee, while chic stores present the newest trends in clothing. Explore independently owned bookshops filled to capacity with worn books or linger in museums that hushed up stories of Portugal's illustrious past. Chiado offers a look into the elegant essence of Lisbon, where history and modernity dance over cobblestone alleyways.

- LX Factory: Industrial Bones Bloom with Creativity:

Explore outside the city's historic center to find LX Factory, a symbol of Lisbon's innovative spirit. This dynamic center, which was once an abandoned industrial zone, is alive with the creative, innovative, and artistic spirit of its residents. Take in a delicious dinner at a chic restaurant located within a former factory, peruse offbeat stores filled with homemade goods, and explore art galleries featuring bold new talents. Lisbon is a city that embraces both its history and its dynamic future, as seen by the way the past and present converge at LX Factory.

- Belém: The City of Sailing Caravels and Sparkling Pastries:

Without a visit to Belém, a district rich in marine exploits, no tour of Lisbon is complete. Imagine the daring adventurers who sailed from this same location, navigating to unexplored seas, as you stand at Belém Tower, a sentinel watching over the entrance of the Tagus River. Enter the Jerónimos Monastery, a magnificent example of Manueline architecture with elaborate sculptures honoring the period of discovery in Portugal. Lastly, savor the delicious Pastel de Nata, a creamy custard dessert that originated in Belém's renowned Pastéis de Belém bakery. This is a must-try Lisbon specialty. History and extravagance converge at Belém, presenting you with a delightful taste of Lisbon's eternal vitality.

This is just a small sampling of the many districts that contribute to Lisbon's vibrancy. Remember that when you explore, the hidden treasures may be found not only on the map but also in the quiet lanes, the sound of laughing coming from a bodega window, or the unexpected run-in with a kind local. So embrace the spirit of exploration, follow your curiosity, and let Lisbon's neighborhoods engross you in their vivid tapestry. Every meeting enhances the symphony of your Lisbon experience, as every corner speaks a fresh narrative and every secret square offers a distinct tune.

CHAPTER FOUR

Iconic landmarks

Lisbon is more than just a collection of monuments; it's a mosaic of tales carved into the stone by the sea's briny murmurs and the sun's golden kisses. Here, famous sites are more than simply tourist attractions; they're vivacious veins pulsating with the history of the city, telling stories of monarchs and explorers and the unwavering spirit of a people who dared to go beyond the horizon. As we go through this tapestry of stone and time, each monument reveals a new thread in Lisbon's enthralling story, so come along, dear traveler.

- Jerónimos Monastery: A Hymn in Stone:

The limestone poetry that is Jerónimos Monastery stands watch on the banks of the Tagus River. Its Manueline style, a colorful fusion of Renaissance and Gothic elements, explodes into detailed carvings that allude to a golden period of exploration and naval victories. Enter and be amazed by the lofty stone vaults that are illuminated by the ethereal light of stained glass windows. Portugal's ambition and creativity are evident in every detail, from the exquisite choir seats to the elaborately carved roof. Here, history is incorporated into the structure itself, not only preserved as a historical footnote.

- Belém Tower: A Sentinel of Dreams:

Proudly standing over the glittering Tagus, Belém Tower is a symbol of Portugal's naval might. Cannons and gargoyles decorate this squat castle, which has seen the departure of innumerable caravels with their sails billowing with hopes of unknown horizons. Imagine Ferdinand Magellan starting his voyage and Vasco da Gama striking out for India, their murmurs blending with the sea air. You can practically hear the murmur of anchor chains and the screams of sailors saying goodbye to their beloved Lisbon as the sun sets and the tower is bathed in a golden hue.

- Castelo São Jorge: A Tale of Two Empires:

São Jorge Castle, perched atop the tallest hill, is a stoic reminder of Lisbon's turbulent history. Roman legions, Moorish invaders, and Portuguese rulers have all passed through its walls, leaving their marks on the worn stones. Discover the maze-like corridors, scale the battlements for expansive views, and feel the ghosts of the past caress your flesh. You will encounter the core of Lisbon's tenacity in this ages-old stronghold—a city that has withstood storms and come out stronger, its soul engraved on each crumbling wall.

- Tram 28: A Time-Traveling Jaunt:

You may travel through time on Lisbon's famous Tram 28, so forget about air-conditioned vehicles. A view into the vibrant core of the city is provided by this dilapidated yellow carriage as it rattles through tiny lanes, past sun-drenched squares and colorful residences. Hold on tight as you make your way across busy streets and steep slopes, grinning at the inhabitants and soaking in the spirit of Lisbon's daily existence. This voyage is more than simply a ride; it's a colorful tapestry stitched on cobblestones, with every creak and groan telling a tale and every turn uncovering a hidden treasure.

- Elevador de Santa Justa: Sending Chiado an Eiffel kiss

Visit the Elevador de Santa Justa to enter a fable. This iron masterpiece, evoking thoughts of the Eiffel Tower, transports you in a fanciful ascension from Baixa Pombal to the chic Chiado area. Lisbon opens out like a map as you ascend above the city, exposing its surprises and mysteries. This elevator is more than simply a means of transportation—its elaborate ironwork and breath-taking views are testaments to Lisbon's creative culture and passion for the dramatic.

- Beyond the Big Names: Hidden Gems Await:

Lisbon's hidden treasures are where the real enchantment is found, even if these well-known sites provide a window into the city's character. For some of the most amazing views of the city, which spreads out like a sun-drenched carpet, go to the Miradouro da Senhora do Monte. Explore the winding alleys of Alfama, where the sad sounds of fado seep from open doors and the passing of time appears to stop. Discover the energetic LX Factory, a refuge for creatives and vintage finds consisting of independent boutiques, hip cafés, and art galleries housed in refurbished warehouses.

Recall that Lisbon's famous sites serve as windows into the spirit of the city, not only as postcards. It is inviting you to explore more and get engrossed in the tapestry of tales woven into its very fabric with every murmur from a worn stone and every echo of a bygone period. Walk with an open mind, follow your curiosity, and explore the secret nooks of Lisbon's enchanted embrace to uncover the enchantment that pulsates inside each famous site and beyond.

CHAPTER FIVE

Culinary delight

Lisbon, located in the center of Portugal, is known for its cuisine and lively culture, which blend together to create a mouthwatering experience. Discovering Lisbon's food scene is a sensory experience that delights the senses with a wide variety of tastes, textures, and scents while exhibiting the mouthwatering options that are firmly anchored in Portuguese culture.

The quintessential Pastéis de Nata is located in the midst of Lisbon's gastronomic wonders. A treasured national dish, these custard tarts have creamy egg custard interiors and crunchy, flaky pastry shells. The most well-known ones are from the legendary Pasteis de Belem, where lines of people waiting to sample these warm, freshly made treats sometimes wrap around the block. But you can have these delicious delicacies in a lot of bakeries and cafés across the city, each bringing an own twist to this irresistible dessert.

Lisbon's markets are a seafood lover's paradise, with the freshest catch of the day tantalizing palates. A seafood lover's dream come true at the lively Mercado da Ribeira, where vendors sell everything from buttery shellfish delicacies to luscious grilled sardines. Lisbon's culinary repertoire revolves on the versatile dish known as bacalhau, or salted fish from Portugal. It is served in a variety of ways that highlight its adaptability.

A trip to Lisbon would not be complete without sampling Petiscos, which are Portuguese tapas served in quaint tascas (taverns). These little but savory plates, such the spicy and smoky sausage called chouriço or the crunchy and flavorful codfish fritters called pataniscas, perfectly capture the spirit of Portuguese cooking. For a really authentic experience, pair these delicious appetizers with a powerful Portuguese red wine or a glass of Vinho Verde.

Lisbon's neighborhoods provide a diverse range of culinary experiences when explored. Travelers are welcome to eat at charming establishments in the ancient Alfama neighborhood that are nestled into little lanes and provide traditional cuisine along with live Fado performances. While everything is going on, the hip Chiado and

Bairro Alto neighborhoods are home to a diverse array of eating options, ranging from hip cafés and rooftop bars to luxury fine dining restaurants that all provide a contemporary take on Portuguese cuisine.

A food tour or cooking lesson may provide a greater insight of Portuguese culinary traditions by revealing the techniques used to create famous meals. Speaking with regional chefs and food specialists may help you get a better understanding of Lisbon's culinary legacy by revealing where ingredients are from, how they are traditionally prepared, and the cultural importance of each dish.

There are possibilities to discover Portugal's wine country on day excursions to the neighboring areas, which are located outside the municipal boundaries. Some of the best wines in the nation are produced in the Douro Valley and Alentejo areas, which are surrounded by rolling vineyards. Gourmet lunches with regional specialties are served with wine tastings and excursions that provide a comprehensive journey into Portugal's winemaking tradition in these stunning surroundings.

Lisbon's culinary offerings are an experience in taste weaving into the city's cultural fabric, not just a means of satisfying hunger. Every meal, rich in invention and history, offers a fascinating window into Portugal's spirit by narrating a tale that goes beyond mere palate pleasure. Savoring Lisbon's culinary gems leaves one with more than just mouthwatering flavors—they also bring back memories of a gastronomic adventure that highlights the diversity of Portuguese cuisine.

Lisbon's culinary tapestry, stitched with strands of heritage, international inspiration, and a splash of bold innovation, shines brighter than ever. Dear Traveler, put aside your old guidebooks and conventional tourist traps and go on a gastronomic journey where Michelin-starred maestros reinvent Portuguese cuisine and new tastes emerge from obscure corners. This serves as your guide to the best restaurants in the city, guaranteeing a sensory overload and a taste experience that will last a lifetime.

- Tradition with a Modern Portuguese Twist:

Albedo: Chef João Rodrigues creates edible paintings in a disused art gallery, drawing inspiration from Portugal's abundant natural resources. Aim for unusual combinations and textures, such as goose barnacles with seaweed ice cream or smoked eel with fig.

The Table of the Rua of the Flowers: Under the direction of chef Hugo Mendes, this iconic bar is being reinvented, bringing back its reputation. Enjoy the duck rice with foie gras, a Portuguese traditional taken to gourmet levels, or try the tuna tataki with avocado and ginger.

Alma: Enter an avant-garde sanctuary where chef Henrique Mouco creates visually stunning meals that highlight fresh produce and local fish. Sea urchin risotto with chorizo and Iberian pig pluma with crispy skin and smoked potato puree are two dishes not to be missed.

- International Cuisine: A Tasty Travel Document:

CENA: Travel around Latin America without ever leaving Lisbon. Chef Pedro Mendes crafts tasting menus including dishes like grilled octopus with passionfruit and pepper or a colorful prawn ceviche with coconut and cashew cream, fusing Portuguese ingredients with Brazilian soul cuisine.

Anima: At Fauna, locally grown vegetables, foraged wild herbs, and meats from ethical sources take center stage. With dishes like wild mushroom risotto with truffle emulsion and charcoal-grilled mackerel with pickled fennel, Chef David Thomas's dishes sigh with sustainability and mindful cooking.

Eleven: Renowned French chef Yannick Alléno, who has received a Michelin star, offers a symphony of traditional French methods and Portuguese fare in Lisbon. Get ready for roasted pigeon with glazed turnips and black truffles, or foie gras terrine with Arbutus honey.

- Hidden Gems and Casual Bites:

Chiado - Cantinho do Avillez: José Avillez's humorous creativity is on full show at Cantinho, a lively tapas bar that is the more laid-back sister of the Michelin-starred Belcanto. Try the pork buns with caramelized pineapple and roasted pig belly, or the bacalhau croquettes with kimchi mayonnaise. You'll be pleasantly pleased.

Pizzarium: This Roman-style pizza heaven in Bairro Alto is the perfect place to satisfy late-night appetites. Your night owl tendencies will be satiated by thin crusts topped with seasonal, fresh ingredients like prosciutto and burrata, which will have you daydreaming of cheesy bliss.

Ribeira Market: This lively market, brimming with vendors highlighting Portugal's gastronomic variety, is a foodie's paradise. Your senses will be overstimulated in the nicest manner possible with everything from exotic fruits and regional cheeses to fresh seafood and delicious sandwiches.

- Exceed the Guidebooks: Seek Your Gastronomic Experience:

Make other maps than Michelin stars your guide. Stumble across a secret tasca offering authentic Portuguese comfort food, such as caldo verde and grilled sardines, while meandering through the picturesque Alfama neighborhood. Find out which "pastelaria" the locals recommend for a sugar rush of flaky pastries and creamy custard tarts. On a backstreet, follow your nose to the smells of grilled chorizo and see the people congregating around a lively tapas bar. Keep in mind that the most delicious finds are often hiding in the cracks and crevices, waiting to astonish and satisfy your daring palette.

- Expert Advice for Lisbon's Gastronomic Scene:

Booking ahead is essential at popular restaurants, particularly on weekends. If obtaining Michelin stars is your objective, make your reservations well in advance to prevent disappointment.

Many restaurants offer terrific value packages (menús do dia) around lunchtime. This is a great chance to taste various meals at a fraction of the cost of à la carte. Don't be afraid to try tiny plates and tapas hopping. Sharing is welcome and a wonderful way to experience the variety of Lisbon's cuisine.

Appreciate your snooze! Make sure to include in the closing hours of many eateries when scheduling your meals.

Ask for suggestions without fear. Most people are glad to recommend their favorite hidden treasures to you.

So, throw away the obsolete menus and bring your spirit of exploration. Lisbon's rich culinary legacy is just waiting to be discovered, mouthful by mouthful. Set off on a culinary adventure where creativity meets tradition, tastes create vivid images, and each dish has a narrative to tell. Just keep in mind that the greatest restaurants in Lisbon are often the ones that are hidden away in quaint alleys, whispered about by kind locals, and just waiting to be found. Cheers to a delicious meal!

Food markets and street eats

Gourmet gems that entice foodies to set out on a gourmet journey may be found right in the center of Lisbon's busy streets. Lisbon's street food and food markets weave together a tapestry of smells, scents, and customs that perfectly capture the spirit of Portuguese cuisine, creating a dynamic culinary culture.

Lisbon's lively food markets, bustling centers of activity where residents and tourists congregate to savor the freshest vegetables, artisanal treats, and real street cuisine, are at the forefront of this gastronomic adventure. Situated in the ancient Cais do Sodré area, the Mercado da Ribeira is a famous marketplace that perfectly captures the essence of Lisbon's culinary culture. A diverse array of vendors provides a plethora of delectable culinary delights, ranging from seafood grills serving freshly caught fish to stands serving authentic Portuguese delicacies.

The perfume of freshly grilled sardines mingles with the smell of spices as one makes their way through the busy aisles of Mercado da Ribeira, luring customers to booths where talented chefs prepare delectable dishes in front of them. People congregate at communal tables to have petiscos, or tiny plates, and to have lively discussions with one another while enjoying in the gastronomic spectacle.

Comparably, the Mercado de Campo de Ourique offers a more secluded environment that is full of character and gastronomic selections. This market has a homey feel to it, with stands brimming with cured meats, organic veggies, handmade cheeses, and mouthwatering pastries. Here, visitors may savor the genuine tastes of Portugal while interacting with artisans who are enthusiastic about what they do, discussing the histories behind their creations and providing samples that capture the spirit of Portuguese cuisine.

But the real heart of Lisbon's food scene is found in its street food, where the character of the city is shown in inexpensive but delicious meals that can be found all over the city in kiosks, food trucks, and traditional tascas.

The ubiquitous scent of freshly made Pastéis de Nata, the famous Portuguese custard tarts, permeates bakeries and street vendors, and it is impossible to ignore. These flaky, golden treats are sprinkled with cinnamon and provide a great combination of creamy custard and crunchy pastry shell, inviting onlookers to indulge in a typical Lisbon pleasure.

Lisbon's streets are full with surprises just waiting to be discovered. Street sellers provide a wide range of cuisines to suit every taste, from substantial Caldo Verde, a classic soup made with kale, potatoes, and chorizo, to luscious pork sandwiches known as "Bifanas," which are laced with garlic and spices.

At dusk, the Bairro Alto neighborhood becomes a hive of street food activity. A dynamic midnight culinary scene is created as narrow alleyways come alive with food vendors offering mouthwatering foods like gourmet burgers, grilled fish, and Prego no Pão (steak sandwiches).

Lisbon's street food events, including the Mercado de Fusão, showcase a blend of foreign and traditional Portuguese foods, celebrating gastronomy's inventiveness and variety. These gatherings provide regional chefs and suppliers a stage on which to display their culinary skills and entice guests to experience a cross-border gastronomic adventure.

Outside of the city center, Belém's historic quarter entices foodies with its famous Pasteis de Belém, which is where the world-famous custard tarts originated. Travelers may enjoy these warm, creamy pastries while taking in the nearby historical monuments and see the painstaking process of manufacturing these delicious pastries, passed down through the years.

Lisbon's food markets and street cuisine provide more than just a taste of the city; they are windows into the city's spirit, where community, creativity, and tradition come together. Enjoying a meal in the heart of the city or on a busy street corner, Lisbon's rich culinary legacy is evident in every mouthful, which also serves as an invitation to experience the sensations that make this dynamic city so unique. These encounters transform into more than just meals as the smells and scents cling to the senses, creating priceless memories of a city rich in culinary grandeur.

CHAPTER SIX

Arts and culture

Lisbon is more than simply a city; it's a work of art with a plethora of creative energy, a stage upon which culture hums in secret passageways and history whispers stories along cobblestone pathways. It is a symphony of spirit, with the sad melodies of fado blending with the beat of street performers, galleries pulsating with the boldness of modern creation, and museums whispering tales of monarchs and explorers. So let go of your preconceptions, traveler, and prepare to be carried away by this colorful tapestry of art and culture.

- Artistic Treasures and Whispers of History: Museums:

Jerónimos Monastery: Enter a work of Manueline architecture, where exquisite sculptures narrate stories of the heyday of Portuguese exploration. Admire the graves of Luís de Camões and Vasco da Gama amid its hallowed corridors, and let the ethereal colors of the stained glass windows wash over you.

National Archaeological Museum: Visit this rich store of cultural legacy to travel through time and see everything from Roman sculptures to Renaissance paintings. Revel in the quiet beauty of Nuno Gonçalves' "Madonna of Belém" or lose yourself in the minute details of Hieronymus Bosch's "Temptations of Saint Anthony."

National Museum of Tile: Explore the fascinating world of azulejos to get an insight into Portugal's colorful character. These vibrant tiles, which cover walls and reveal secrets at every turn, tell the narrative of the city via Moorish inspirations and modern reinterpretations.

- Art Pours Into the Streets: Beyond the Walls:

LX Factory: This former industrial area has been transformed into a creative hub. Explore galleries with striking modern art, look around oddball design stores, and have coffee in hip cafés converted from disused factories.

Murals of Street Art: Watch closely, as Lisbon's streets are a dynamic work of art.

These murals, which range from charming color splashes to provocative political stencils, bring the city's tales to life in unexpected places and vividly depict its history.

Fado Houses: The gloomy fado tunes of Alfama give expression to Lisbon's soul. Bask in the warm glow of candlelight as you lose yourself in cozy pubs where heartfelt singers share tales of saudade, love, and grief.

- Literary Interests and Dramatic Pleasures:

São Carlos National Theatre: Enter a world of exquisite acoustics and captivating theatrical productions. Plays, ballets, and operas are presented at this ancient theater, providing an insight into Portuguese performing arts.

Livraria Bertrand: Get lost in the world's oldest bookstore's maze-like aisles. Established in 1740, this literary treasure trove has ages' worth of tales, muttering about the great writers of Portugal and beckoning you to take a literary journey of your own.

Events and Festivals: Use the city as a stage! Lisbon is a year-round energy hub, from the exuberant Carnival events to the immersive Festa de Santo António. Become a part of the vivid fabric of the city by immersing yourself in the music, dancing, and customs.

- Surprises and Innovative Turning Points:

Embaixada: This autonomous art venue, located in a historic palace, pushes the frontiers of creativity and ignites conversation with its thought-provoking exhibits, performances, and discussions.

Ribeira Market: Experience the vibrant food scene of the city at this bustling market. Savor locally produced goods, indulge in delicious food, and take in the creative mood as musicians and entertainers enliven the already lively scene.

Miradouros: Scale one of Lisbon's numerous miradouros, or overlooks, to get a panoramic perspective that encapsulates the essence of the city. See the terracotta roofs tumbling down the hills, watch the sun paint the Tagus River with flaming colors, and let the spirit of the city wash over you.

Remember that Lisbon's arts and culture are not limited to theaters and museums; they are found dancing in the city's light, pulsating in its alleys and echoing in its music. So take a stroll with an open mind, follow your curiosity, and enjoy Lisbon's soulful symphony. In this city where musicians play for your walks, artists paint your steps, and every cobblestone speaks a tale, get involved, don't simply watch. Art is something to experience, breathe, and live in Lisbon, not simply something to look at.

Wanderer, go out and let Lisbon's colorful tapestry of arts and culture to enchant you inside.

Theatres and performances

Theatrical arts flourish in Lisbon's dynamic metropolis in a seductive fusion of history, creativity, and cultural diversity. The city presents a wide range of shows that captivate spectators and honor the deep meaning of creative expression. Lisbon's theaters and performances are profound expressions of the city's character, where history and modern inventiveness blend to create a tapestry of dramatic talent, music, dance, and narrative that captivates audiences.

The Teatro Nacional D. Maria II, a stunning building in Rossio Square, is the focal point of Lisbon's theater scene. Rich in history and opulence, this magnificent theater presents a diverse range of events, from avant-garde performances to traditional plays, acting as a stronghold for Portuguese dramatic arts. The lavish auditorium and the elaborately detailed interiors create a magical atmosphere that carries viewers into a world where theatrical magic is realized.

Teatro Nacional D. Maria II offers a wide range of musical selections all year long to suit a variety of palates. The theatre embraces a blend of genres and tales that appeal to both local audiences and worldwide theater fans, showcasing anything from timeless works by famous Portuguese authors to adaptations of foreign classics. It acts as a cultural lighthouse, encouraging discussion and thought via the performing arts' prism.

Lisbon's theater culture embraces non-traditional venues that provide performers a fresh perspective in addition to conventional stages. Nestled in Alfama area, the Chapitô is a unique circus-theater that epitomizes invention and inventiveness. This vibrant space blends live music, drama, and circus arts, enthralling viewers with its unique productions that defy expectations of what constitutes traditional performance art.

In addition, Lisbon's musical landscape is a lively patchwork of melodies and beats that accentuate the city's theatrical attractions. Intimate settings like Clube de Fado resound with the profound Portuguese music genre of fado, where gifted musicians and vocalists conjure genuine emotions, taking listeners to the depths of Portuguese sorrow and love.

The Calouste Gulbenkian Foundation, a cultural organization that supports modern dance performances, art exhibits, and classical music concerts, is another example of the city's dedication to supporting creative expression. Lisbon's cultural tapestry is enhanced by the harmonic fusion of classical and contemporary creative undertakings performed on its auditorium stage by world-class musicians, orchestras, and dancers.

Lisbon also supports events honoring the performing arts, which attract visitors and performers from all over the globe. Renowned worldwide performing arts event Alkantara event presents innovative dance, theater, and performance art at several locations across the city, providing a forum for discussion and cross-cultural interaction.

Lisbon's nightlife comes alive with a plethora of entertainment alternatives as day turns into night. Historically referred to as the city's entertainment area, the landmark Parque Mayer is home to a variety of theaters, cabarets, and music halls that present a wide range of productions, from comedies to musicals, appealing to a wide range of people.

Spaces like Teatro do Bairro, a platform that promotes new playwrights, directors, and actors and creates a dynamic setting for creative and thought-provoking plays, are examples of the city's dedication to developing emerging talent.

Lisbon's theaters and performing venues embrace innovation while retaining legacy, acting as cultural ambassadors in addition to providing entertainment. They provide a forum for creative expression, encouraging discussion, reflection, and a greater understanding of the human condition.

The dynamic theatrical scene of the city takes viewers on a voyage of discovery, with every show serving as a monument to the influence of the arts and the storytelling medium. Lisbon's theaters and performances produce a symphony of emotions, leaving lasting impressions on the hearts and minds of those who indulge in their magical embrace. These impressions range from the grandeur of ancient theaters to the avant-garde attempts in unorthodox locations.

Arts galleries and exhibition

Lisbon's art galleries and exhibits provide a kaleidoscope of creative expressions that fascinate, inspire, and elicit thought. They serve as colorful representations of the city's cultural diversity. Lisbon's art scene is a fascinating tapestry that honors originality, innovation, and the wide range of visual arts, spanning from ancient institutions to modern venues.

The Museu Nacional de Arte Antiga (National Museum of Ancient Art) is a magnificent architectural structure located in the center of Lisbon's creative district. It is home to a significant collection of centuries-old Portuguese and European art. Here, guests go on a visual voyage through time and come across works of art by well-known painters like Nuno Gonçalves, Albrecht Dürer, and Hieronymus Bosch. The striking collection of decorative arts, paintings, and sculptures at the museum invites reflection on creative development and historical narratives while providing a window into Portugal's cultural past.

A haven for art lovers is the cultural institution Fundação Calouste Gulbenkian, which is tucked away among verdant gardens. The museum has a diverse collection that includes European artworks, Islamic art, antiques, and a remarkable collection of Lalique jewelry. The modern art center, which hosts contemporary exhibits and promotes conversation between tradition and innovation, is another example of the foundation's dedication to advancing cross-cultural interchange.

Lisbon's creative appeal extends beyond conventional museum settings, encompassing cutting-edge contemporary art galleries that challenge conventions. Known for its creative energy, the Chiado neighborhood is home to galleries like Galeria Ratton and Galeria Belo-Galsterer, which display avant-garde pieces by well-known and up-and-coming artists. These galleries include a variety of media and conceptual art that subvert stereotypes and provoke thought, acting as breeding grounds for creative innovation.

In addition, the vibrant creative center known as the LX Factory, housed in a former industrial building, is a hive of artistic activity. It is home to galleries like Ler Devagar, an unorthodox bookshop and exhibition space decorated with amusing sculptures and creative installations, and Underdogs Gallery, which specializes in urban art and modern illustration. Lisbon's culture of welcoming innovation and reusing venues to support creative expression is personified by The LX Factory.

Institutions like the MAAT (Museum of Art, Architecture, and Technology), a modern architectural wonder with a view of the Tagus River, are examples of Lisbon's dedication to fostering contemporary art. MAAT hosts exhibits that explore multidisciplinary subjects and engage audiences via immersive installations and thought-provoking displays, all while seamlessly integrating art, architecture, and technology.

Annual events like as ARCOlisboa, an international contemporary art market that brings together artists, galleries, and collectors from all over the globe, contribute to the city's thriving art scene. Through the exhibition of cutting-edge works and the promotion of links within the international art community, this event turns Lisbon into a center of creative interchange.

Lisbon's cultural environment is further enhanced by the unexpected and impromptu nature of its street art culture. The city's walls are canvases for regional and global street artists, who embellish residential areas like Bairro Alto and Alfama with colorful murals and provocative graffiti, transforming the urban environment into an outdoor art gallery.

Lisbon's art is more than just beautiful; it is a mirror reflecting the essence of the city, its past, and its present. It encourages guests to participate in an interlingual visual dialogue by providing a range of viewpoints, thought-provoking discussions, and evoking strong emotions.

In addition to showcasing creative talent, Lisbon's galleries and exhibits act as forums for cross-cultural dialogue, promoting relationships between creators, viewers, and concepts. Each piece of art serves as a window into the artist's vision and a reflection of the complex nature of human expression, inviting viewers to go on an exploratory journey.

Art serves as a medium for reflection, inspiration, and admiration of the deep beauty found in the creative and imaginative domains of Lisbon's galleries and exhibits. Traveling through these areas immerses tourists in a symphony of cross-border creative storylines that leave a lasting impression on Lisbon's cultural landscape.

CHAPTER SEVEN

Outdoor activities

Lisbon is more than simply a city of cobblestone streets and pastel facades; it is a city hugged by the Tagus River and caressed by the sun. It's a painting filled with colorful outdoor activities just waiting to be explored, a playground for energetic people. So, adventurer, kick off your city shoes and put on your sneakers since Lisbon offers a wide variety of activities that go far beyond the bounds of tourist attractions and museums.

- Breathe the ocean, embrace the river:

Sail into Sunset: Take a Tagus River sunset cruise to see Lisbon paint itself in flaming colors. Enjoy a glass of sangria while watching the city skyline turn to dusk, feel the breeze in your hair, and allow the soft rocking transport you to a blissful state of mind.

Surf's Up!: Praia do Guincho is a surfer's paradise located just outside of Lisbon. Catch some waves there. There are lots of instructors and board rentals available, regardless of your experience level as a shredder. Enjoy the rush of riding the energy of the ocean, bask in the golden light, and put your troubles down on the sand.

Time Traveling Kayak: Kayaking around Belém Bay's serene waters will take you on a historical voyage. As you float through time, paddle by famous sites like Belém Tower and Jerónimos Monastery, whispering stories of explorers and conquistadors.

- Trails and Hills: A Place Where Nature Calls:

Tram 28 Hike: Take a physical journey along the famed Tram 28 route to escape the throng. Walk along its route via little alleyways and secret passageways, taking in expansive city vistas and coming across undiscovered treasures. Grab a picnic basket, choose a location in the sun, and take in the city from a new angle.

Monsanto Forest Escape: Visit Monsanto Forest Park to take in the fresh air and get away from the bustle of the city. Discover secret waterfalls, take a hike through pine woods and eucalyptus groves, and feel the city melt away under your feet. Bring your mountain bike for more excitement, or just stroll along the meandering paths and enjoy the peace.

The Enchanted Hills of Sintra: Explore the fanciful paradise of Sintra by traveling outside of Lisbon. tour the Moorish Castelo dos Mouros, take a walk through the ethereal Pena National Palace grounds, or tour the Pena National Palace on foot. Every turn opens up a fresh view, and every wind whisper recalls a past tale.

- City Rides and City Explorations:

Two Wheels, Unlimited Discovery: Hire a bike and ride through the colorful mosaic that is Lisbon. Cruise the promenade along the Tagus River, explore secret squares brimming with local activity, and meander through quaint passageways. Take a map and a spirit of adventure with you, and let the city lead the way on two wheels.

Cache Adventure: Treasure Hunt: Use geocaching to transform Lisbon into an interactive playground. Get the app, solve the puzzles, and open the secret caches strewn over the city. You will find hidden spots, historical sites, and breath-taking vistas that you would not otherwise find on this technological treasure hunt.

City Art Tour: Take your camera and go on a safari through street art. Lisbon's city walls are covered with colorful murals, wacky stencils, and provocative graffiti. Explore Bairro Alto and LX Factory, look for hidden gems, and document every moment of the city's creative energy.

- Take Up the Local Lifestyle:

Park Picnic: Take a bottle of vinho verde and a basket full of regional specialties to a sun-filled area in one of Lisbon's numerous parks. Unwind in the shade of the trees, take in the ambience, and observe the passing folks. The ideal getaways from the bustle of the city are Eduardo VII Park, Tapada da Ajuda, or Jardim da Estrela.

Participate in the Festas: Take in the lively atmosphere of Lisbon during one of its numerous festivals. The city is a flurry of song, dancing, and joyful celebration, from the boisterous Santo António festivities in June to the vibrant Carnival in February. Take part in the parades, try some street cuisine, and let the contagious enthusiasm to envelope you.

Sunset Sips: Enjoy a sunset beverage at one of Lisbon's numerous miradouros (viewpoints) to round off your outdoor excursion. As the city is bathed in golden colors, have a cool drink, watch as one by one the glittering lights ignite, and let Lisbon's beauty to seep into your spirit.

Keep in mind that Lisbon's natural playground isn't limited to parks and tourist routes. There is adventure to be found on every cobblestone street, every secret lane, and every rooftop patio. Therefore, go with an open mind and an inquisitive heart since the most thrilling discoveries are often found off the map, just waiting to be discovered by daring individuals. Put on some sunscreen, tighten your shoes, and enjoy Lisbon's colorful array of outdoor activities.

Parks and gardens

Amidst Lisbon's busy streets and old districts are lush green spaces that provide relaxation, peace, and stunning views of the surrounding landscape. Lisbon's parks and gardens are more than simply verdant areas; they are enchanted retreats that invite both inhabitants and tourists to lose themselves in the embrace of nature, promoting a well-balanced mix of leisure, entertainment, and cultural enhancement.

Parque Eduardo VII, a vast park with expansive views of Lisbon and the Tagus River, is located in the center of the city. Dedicated to England's King Edward VII, this vast green area has well-kept lawns, colorful flowerbeds, and meandering walkways that encourage strolls. The park's calm atmosphere is livened up by a variety of activities, such as outdoor exhibits and music festivals.

Jardim da Estrela is a charming garden oasis with a serene aura that is located not far from the city center. This charming park is surrounded by wrought-iron gates and has a playground, exotic plants, and tall palms along its center pond, which is home to ducks and swans. The centerpiece of the park is the Estrela Basilica, a lavish church whose imposing dome enhances its charm and makes it a popular location for relaxed picnics and introspective times.

Lisbon's green tapestry is further enhanced by the Tapada das Necessidades, a hidden jewel rich in floral grandeur and history. This vast park, which was once a royal estate, enthralls guests with its serene ambiance, rich gardens, and wide variety of plant life. Magnificent fountains, serene ponds, and stately mansions all contribute to the park's allure, making it the perfect place for leisurely strolls and admiration of its architectural and natural beauties.

Lisbon is committed to protecting its natural heritage, and this is evident in the charming Parque Florestal de Monsanto, the biggest urban park in Europe. Tucked away in a wooded setting, this large park is a paradise for nature lovers with hiking trails, bike lanes, and picnic areas that provide amazing views over the city. It is a well-liked location for both residents and visitors looking for outdoor experiences because of its varied flora and fauna as well as recreational amenities.

Lisbon's botanical gardens are also live examples of horticultural beauty and biodiversity. Offering a window into the richness of tropical flora, the Jardim Botânico Tropical (Tropical Botanical Garden) welcomes guests to discover a world of unusual plants from former Portuguese territories. In the meanwhile, the Ajuda National Palace's neighbor, the Jardim Botânico da Ajuda (Ajuda Botanical Garden), enthralls with its well chosen plant collections, peaceful walkways, and historical importance.

Initiatives like the Gulbenkian Gardens, a division of the Calouste Gulbenkian Foundation, which skillfully combine art, architecture, and nature, demonstrate the city's dedication to protecting green areas. These gardens function as a cultural center, presenting outdoor concerts, art exhibits, and exhibitions that enhance the park experience. They are embellished with sculptures, peaceful water elements, and an outdoor amphitheater.

Lisbon's riverbank promenades, which extend beyond the boundaries of conventional parks, provide breathtaking views and leisure activities. Designed for Expo '98, the Parque das Nações has the riverbank Vasco da Gama Park, where guests may take leisurely strolls, bike rides, and dine by the riverfront while taking in the contemporary architecture and public art displays.

Lisbon's parks and gardens are peaceful havens away from the bustle of the city, where history, culture, and leisure coexist with nature. In addition to offering areas for leisure and enjoyment, these green sanctuaries stand as live examples of Lisbon's dedication to protecting its natural legacy for future generations. Wandering through these picture-perfect settings, tourists find refuges where the rich tapestry of the city and the beauty of nature combine to provide life-changing experiences that uplift the spirit, body, and mind.

Biking tours

An exciting and engaging way to see Lisbon's lively districts, iconic sites, and breathtaking landscapes is via bike excursions. These excursions, which include the city's rolling hills, quaint neighborhoods, and stunning waterfronts, provide a journey that blends sightseeing with an active, environmentally conscious experience, letting visitors explore Lisbon's essence at their own speed.

Biking in Lisbon is a fascinating experience since it offers you the chance to see its famous sites and varied districts. Riding through the cobblestone lanes of Alfama, the oldest area, cyclists begin in the historic center and wind through small alleyways filled with the aroma of local food and the sounds of Fado music. Cycling up towards

São Jorge Castle, which sits atop one of Lisbon's seven hills, rewards riders with sweeping views of the Tagus River sparkling and the city's red roofs. This climb provides an unmatched perspective of Lisbon's spectacular landscapes.

Along the riverbank, bike rides reveal Lisbon's maritime history by following the banks of the Tagus River. Bicyclists follow the riverfront promenade through the Belém area, taking in the architectural magnificence and the cool wind coming from the water. The neighborhood is home to famous buildings like the Jerónimos Monastery and the Belém Tower.

Biking trips in Lisbon are now both accessible and pleasurable because to the city's dedication to improving the bicycle infrastructure. The city is lined with bike lanes that are specifically designed to make riding safe and enjoyable. Along the journey, participants may choose between paths according to their ability level, with trained guides providing information about Lisbon's hidden treasures, history, and culture.

Bike rides in Lisbon can help visitors develop a closer relationship with everyday life and local culture. They provide chances to discover lively marketplaces, handcrafted stores, and quaint cafés along the streets. During their breaks, riders may have Portuguese coffee or experience the traditional Pastéis de Nata while taking in the vibrant environment of the surrounding districts.

These trips often stop at viewpoints and lesser-known locations, giving visitors the chance to take in breathtaking views and unearth hidden gems that could be overlooked on more conventional excursions. Miradouro da Senhora do Monte and Miradouro de Santa Catarina are two examples of vistas, or miradouros, that provide stunning panoramic views of Lisbon and are ideal for contemplative times and photos.

Biking trips depart from the city center and go into Lisbon's suburbs and natural areas, providing a change of scenery from the city. Bicyclists appreciate the routes that meander through forested sections as they explore the verdant surroundings of Monsanto Forest Park, offering a peaceful diversion from the bustle of the city while savoring the splendor of nature.

In addition, electric bike tours are becoming more and more well-liked since they let users explore Lisbon's mountainous terrain with ease and benefit from assisted pedaling. All physical levels are catered for on these trips, so visitors can easily cover the city's distances and hills without overdoing it.

Biking excursions in Lisbon provide guests the freedom to personalize their experience. Riders may customize their schedule and see Lisbon at their own speed by choosing self-guided tours utilizing bike-sharing services or group excursions with experienced guides.

Themed bicycling experiences, including food-focused tours or sunset rides along the riverbank, give new views on Lisbon's culinary pleasures or the city's lovely atmosphere as the sun sets. These experiences are available in addition to the everyday excursions.

Lisbon biking tours are more than simply sightseeing; they represent a fully immersed experience that stimulates the senses, encourages discovery, and produces lifelong memories. Biking in Lisbon is a fantastic way to experience the city's charm, uncovering its treasures and revealing a side of the city that is both energizing and enriching. It combines physical exercise, cultural immersion, and scenic beauty.

CHAPTER EIGHT

Accommodation

Lisbon has a broad range of lodging alternatives to meet any traveler's interests, from opulent hotels to quaint guesthouses and affordable hostels. The lodgings are as dynamic and varied as the city itself. Lisbon, one of Europe's most alluring travel destinations, greets guests with a hospitality scene that embodies the city's warm Portuguese hospitality, modern flare, and rich historical legacy.

Redefining extravagance, luxury hotels in Lisbon provide impeccable style and top-notch facilities. Elegant establishments with rich decor, breathtaking vistas, Michelin-starred restaurants, spas, and first-rate service are the epitome of sophistication. Examples of these properties include the Four Seasons Hotel Ritz Lisbon and the Tivoli Avenida Liberdade. These facilities appeal to discriminating guests seeking exclusivity and pleasure by effortlessly fusing contemporary conveniences with classic charm.

Lisbon's boutique hotels provide a wealth of personality and charm for those looking for a more private and tailored stay. With its distinctive designs, handcrafted artwork, and customized services, hotels such as the Memmo Alfama Hotel and the Santiago de Alfama Boutique Hotel encapsulate the spirit of Lisbon's districts and provide a homey feel even when guests are not there. These boutique hotels let visitors fully experience Lisbon's genuine atmosphere by showcasing the city's culture and legacy.

In addition, Lisbon's bed & breakfasts and guesthouses radiate warmth and genuineness. Places like the Lisbonaire Apartments and Casa Balthazar, which are charming and friendly, provide comfortable lodging that combines comfort with regional charm. Personalized attention, insider knowledge from amiable hosts, and distinctive touches that make every visit unforgettable are common features of these guesthouses.

Lisbon's hostels and low-cost lodging alternatives are many for budget travelers. Trendy hostels featuring active common areas, social events, and opportunities to meet other visitors include The

Independente Hostel & Suites and Yes! Lisbon Hostel. These hostels provide reasonably priced dormitory-style rooms or private accommodations. These reasonably priced choices are well situated in the center of the city, making exploring easy and accessible.

Lisbon also has holiday homes and flats that are ideal for families, groups, or those looking for a more intimate experience. With a vast selection of lodging options available on websites like Airbnb and Vrbo, visitors can live like locals and take their time exploring the city. Cozy apartments in historic areas and roomy villas with panoramic views are just a few of the options available.

Lisbon's housing options can accommodate a range of tastes, from sustainable motels that emphasize environmental responsibility to eco-friendly stays. Eco-friendly lodging options, such as the Inspira Santa Marta Hotel and The Lumiares Hotel & Spa, provide visitors with an opportunity to lessen their carbon footprint without sacrificing comfort or design.

When selecting a place to stay in Lisbon, location is important. The areas of Chiado and Baixa provide a convenient central location with quick access to food options, shopping, and significant attractions. Alfama and Bairro Alto, on the other hand, provide an insight into Lisbon's past and lively nightlife, presenting a more conventional and free-spirited aspect of the city.

Lisbon's lodgings embrace its cultural legacy while reflecting the city's international appeal. Travelers seeking elegance, authenticity, affordability, or a combination of experiences will find Lisbon to be accommodating to a wide range of preferences, making it possible for any visitor to find a place to call home while visiting this fascinating city.

Hotels

As Janelas Verdes Inn, a Lisbon Heritage Collection

Location: Rua das Janelas Verdes, 47, Lisbon 1200-690 Portugal

As Janelas Verdes Inn, a member of the prestigious Lisbon Heritage Collection, is tucked away inside the historic tapestry of Lisbon and takes you on a trip through time and culture while providing an outstanding 4-star stay in the center of Portugal's capital city.

Situated in the quaint Santos neighborhood, this boutique hotel combines elegance and history in an abundance. You are welcomed with a cozy, historic atmosphere as soon as you enter the inn. Every nook whispers stories of the city's history, and the kind personnel sets the mood for an immersive encounter in a bygone age with a true Portuguese welcome.

Each of the apartments at As Janelas Verdes exudes a feeling of refined elegance and is furnished with traditional pieces, luxurious textiles, and elaborate details that honor the cultural past of Lisbon. Enjoy views of the lush gardens or the peaceful Tagus River from the comfort of your hotel, which provides a peaceful haven from the hustle and bustle of the city.

Savor the inn's commitment to comfort and genuineness while visiting. Savor a delicious breakfast buffet that highlights regional specialties and handmade sweets, creating the ideal atmosphere for a day of discovery in Lisbon's ancient districts.

Explore the neighborhood's cobblestone streets, which are home to quaint stores and a bustling street scene. Enjoy leisurely walks along the promenade by the river or discover hidden jewels like the National Ancient Art Museum, which is close by and has a wealth of artifacts that depict historical events in Portugal.

For those seeking a quick city getaway or a longer cultural immersion, As Janelas Verdes provides a comfortable and traditional experience. Because of the inn's dedication to protecting Lisbon's history, you can be confident that your stay will be a flawless blend of elegance and authenticity.

As the Lisbon Heritage Collection's Janelas Verdes Inn extends a warm welcome to an enchanted hideaway where history is enacted and every little detail embodies Lisbon's character. Savor the charms of this four-star sanctuary, where the past and modern collide, guaranteeing a memorable stay in the center of Lisbon's vibrant cultural scene.

Hotel Ibis Lisboa Jose Malhoa

Location: Avenida Jose Malhoa Lote H, Lisbon 1070-158 Portugal

Discover the luxury of contemporary minimalism at the 3-star Hotel Ibis Lisboa Jose Malhoa, a modern sanctuary ideally located in the energetic center of Lisbon.

Tucked away in the heart of the commercial sector, this chic hotel greets you with friendliness and efficiency. Upon entering the lobby, you will experience a smooth check-in procedure together with the authentic friendliness that epitomizes the Ibis brand. The welcoming staff members set the tone for a hassle-free and enjoyable stay with their sincere smiles, which guarantee a seamless welcome.

The Hotel Ibis Lisboa Jose Malhoa's rooms are the perfect combination of comfort and usefulness. With its modern style, each room provides a comfortable haven where you can rest after seeing Lisbon for the day. The contemporary facilities attend to your requirements and provide a soothing ambiance to revitalize you for the adventures of the following day.

Savor the hotel's handy location, which makes it simple to see Lisbon's cultural attractions throughout your visit. Discovering the city is a breeze with the hotel's close location to major attractions and public transit, whether you're here for a quick city break or a long business trip.

Savor the lively local food scene or go for a quick walk to Eduardo VII Park, which offers luscious flora and expansive city vistas. Thanks to the hotel's convenient location, you can fully immerse yourself in Lisbon's vibrant environment, uncovering its hidden treasures and taking in its genuine charm.

More than simply a place to sleep, Hotel Ibis Lisboa Jose Malhoa serves as a doorway to all of Lisbon's excitement and vibrancy. In the center of Lisbon's busy environment, embrace the comfort and convenience of our 3-star refuge, where contemporary meets utility to ensure a pleasurable stay.

Bairro Alto Hotel

Location: Praca Luis de Camoes 2, Lisbon 1200-243 Portugal

The elegant Bairro Alto Hotel, a boutique five-star jewel that captures the spirit of the city's bohemian energy and modern elegance, is perched in the center of Lisbon's bustling Bairro Alto area.

A feeling of chic elegance welcomes you as soon as you enter the hotel's elegant lobby, luring you into an opulent and cozy environment. The welcoming staff, with their friendly and professional demeanor, sets the stage for an unmatched stay full of Lisbon's enthralling charm.

The Bairro Alto Hotel's rooms are each carefully crafted to combine contemporary elegance with a hint of regional history, creating a haven of exquisite luxury. Luxurious furniture, tasteful design, and breathtaking views of Lisbon's charming streets all contribute to an atmosphere that exudes exquisite calm.

During your visit, the hotel serves as your entryway to explore Bairro Alto's essence. Take in the lively vibe of the neighborhood's buzzing bars, stroll through the colorful lanes decorated with street art, and enjoy in the diverse food scene that highlights Lisbon's culinary delicacies.

Enjoy a lovely breakfast that is served against a stunning panorama of Lisbon dawning on a new day, all from the hotel's patio. Enjoy leisurely walks to neighboring cultural monuments like the São Pedro de Alcântara viewpoint or explore the surrounding medieval Chiado area.

Whether you're staying for a long weekend or a longer visit, the Bairro Alto Hotel guarantees a remarkable time. Take in the hotel's unwavering dedication to quality, where every little thing—from individualized service to carefully chosen experiences—guarantees an experience that goes above and beyond your expectations.

The 5-star Bairro Alto Hotel, a shining example of refinement and elegance in the center of Lisbon, cordially welcomes you to experience a luxurious stay that expertly combines extravagance with the genuineness of Portuguese culture. Amidst the dynamic energy and timeless beauty of Bairro Alto, get ready for an amazing stay that will fascinate you.

Resorts

Lisbon's historic beauty and cultural appeal entice visitors, but the city's suburbs also include a variety of opulent resorts that contrast with the urban liveliness of the area by providing tranquil surroundings and top-notch facilities.

With its locations tucked away along the coast or in the heart of lush countryside, Lisbon's resorts exemplify luxury and leisure. These places provide a peaceful sanctuary that perfectly combines luxury, scenic splendor, and first-rate service.

Resort Penha Longa - The Penha Longa Resort, with the breathtaking Sintra Mountains as a background, provides a getaway into verdant surroundings and classic elegance. This sumptuous hideaway has a championship golf course, an exquisite spa, and sophisticated lodgings. Visitors may take in the tranquility of the resort's lovely surrounds or visit the neighboring UNESCO World Heritage Site of Sintra.

- The Oitavos - The Oitavos, a modern masterpiece that combines stunning views of the Atlantic Ocean with contemporary design, is nestled among Cascais's natural beauty. A championship golf course, a holistic wellness center, and a variety of outdoor sports including surfing and horseback riding are all available to visitors at this five-star resort.

- Algarve Conrad - Although it's not in Lisbon itself, the Conrad Algarve, the height of luxury in Portugal's south, is not far from the city. This gorgeous resort, located in the Algarve, offers perfect service and a tranquil atmosphere. With its luxurious spa, Michelin-starred restaurants, and gorgeous accommodations, the Conrad Algarve is the perfect getaway for anyone looking for a little luxury and leisure.

Numerous of these resorts provide as entry points for seeing the areas around Lisbon. All while returning to the lap of luxury at the end of the day, they provide chances to explore the gorgeous beaches along the coastline, journey into the charming villages of Cascais and Sintra, or learn more about Portugal's natural treasures and rich history.

These resorts provide a smooth blend of luxury, relaxation, and discovery while providing a respite from the bustle of the metropolis. They embody the perfect balance of leisure and exploration, enhancing Lisbon's metropolitan allure with their unmatched friendliness and breathtaking surroundings. In the midst of Portugal's breathtaking scenery, Lisbon's resorts provide a remarkable and opulent experience for anyone looking for a golf getaway, spa treat, or just a peaceful getaway.

Camping sites

Camping aficionados will find a wide variety of charming campsites in and around Lisbon that combine outdoor adventure, natural beauty, and close proximity to the city's cultural treasures. These camping areas provide a peaceful haven for those who want to take in Portugal's breathtaking scenery with convenient access to the energetic metropolis of Lisbon.

- Camping & Bungalows Lisboa:

Lisboa Camping & Bungalows is an urban sanctuary offering a distinctive camping experience, tucked away in the center of Lisbon. This campground, which is part of Monsanto Forest Park, provides a peaceful fusion of convenience and environment.

Campers may pitch their tents among the verdant surroundings, only a short distance from the heart of Lisbon. In addition, Lisboa Camping offers furnished tents and bungalows for those who want a more pleasant stay. The location is perfect for families or anyone seeking a blend of urban and natural adventure since it has contemporary amenities including playgrounds, a swimming pool, and Wi-Fi.

- Camping Costa da Caparica:

Costa da Caparica Camping is the ideal getaway for beach enthusiasts, located only a short distance from Caparica's breathtaking beaches. This campground, which faces the Atlantic Ocean, lets guests wake up to the tranquil sounds of the waves. Guests have the option of staying in cozy bungalows or setting up camp on sand dunes with their campers or tents. The beach is conveniently close to the campground, making seaside picnics, surfing, and sunbathing regular activities. This campsite is a great place to unwind by the sea, and there are eateries nearby that provide fresh seafood.

- Piedense Campismo Park:

Nestled by the Tagus River in Seixal, only a short boat ride from Lisbon, Parque de Campismo Piedense provides a peaceful haven. This campground, which is surrounded by nature, offers roomy campsites for tents and campers along with cozy cottages. The location offers features including a restaurant that serves authentic Portuguese food, a swimming pool, and areas for outdoor recreation like fishing and kayaking. Hiking routes, seeing the neighboring towns, or just relaxing while taking in expansive views of the river and the skyline of Lisbon are all available to visitors.

- Guincho Orbitur:

The unmatched camping experience at Orbitur Guincho, near Cascais, is ideal for nature lovers seeking adventure and stunning scenery. This campground is tucked away in the Sintra-Cascais Natural Park, surrounded by verdant pine trees and close to the breathtaking Guincho Beach. While taking advantage of the cool sea air and participating in outdoor pursuits like hiking, cycling, or windsurfing, campers may set up their tents or park their caravans. A grocery, a bar, and playgrounds are just a few of the facilities the location offers, appealing to both families and outdoor lovers.

- Alenquer Camping:

Located about 45 minutes from Lisbon in the quaint village of Alenquer, Camping Alenquer provides a tranquil rural environment surrounded by vineyards and undulating hills. For those looking for a quiet and rustic camping experience, this campground is the perfect getaway. Campers may benefit from large plots, grilling areas, and a shared kitchen. In addition, the location provides opportunities for hiking, horseback riding, and birding, letting guests experience the peace and quiet of the Portuguese countryside.

These camping locations close to Lisbon provide a variety of experiences, accommodating a range of tastes and serving as a starting point for seeing the area's natural beauties while enjoying the conveniences of outdoor life. Lisbon's camping sites provide an enthralling and engaging way to enjoy the splendor of Portugal's landscapes, whether you're looking for quiet rural escape, city closeness, or coastal leisure.

CHAPTER NINE

Language and communication tips

Knowing your way about a foreign city like Lisbon may be a rewarding experience, particularly if you are aware of certain important vocabulary and communication guidelines. You may make the most of your stay and your encounters with the friendly people of Lisbon by becoming involved in the local language and culture. Make the most of your stay in the city with these excellent language and communication ideas.

- Learn Basic Portuguese Phrases:

Even though English is widely spoken in Lisbon, it might still be beneficial to pick up a few simple Portuguese words to establish rapport and demonstrate appreciation for the local way of life. Easy salutations like as

"Olá" (hello), "Por favor" (please), and "Obrigado/a" (thank you) may have a big impact on how you interact with others.

- Embrace the Politeness of Portuguese Culture:

Portuguese culture places a great importance on politeness. Good manners and respect are shown by using phrases like "Com licença" (pardon me), "Bom dia" (good morning), "Boa tarde" (good afternoon), and "Boa noite" (good evening/night), which promote constructive conversation.

- Communicate Clearly and Slowly:

For natives who may not speak English as their first language, speaking slowly and clearly may be quite beneficial. It guarantees more seamless communication and helps with understanding.

- Employ Body Language and Gestures:

Language difficulties may be supplemented by nonverbal communication, such as hand gestures and facial expressions. But be aware of how gestures fluctuate depending on the culture; some may indicate different things in Portugal than they do back home.

- Request Help:

Never be afraid to seek for assistance if you run across linguistic problems. Lisbon residents are generally amiable and eager to help tourists. Ask them nicely whether they can assist you with basic English terms or if they speak English.

- Employ Translation Applications:

When faced with language barriers, carrying a pocket-sized phrasebook or using translation apps might be helpful. Technology has facilitated communication by enabling real-time translation and overcoming linguistic divides.

- Take Part in Cultural Events:

Engaging in local activities offers an immersive experience. Examples of these activities include going on guided tours, going to cultural events, or visiting traditional markets. You may converse with locals and get more knowledge about their language, traditions, and way of life by doing so.

- Exercise patience and mindfulness:

It takes both patience and an open mind to communicate in a foreign language. Make errors; it's okay to make mistakes; the people you attempt to communicate with in their language will appreciate it.

- Honor regional traditions and customs:

Respecting regional cultures and customs is essential to productive communication. Respecting and observing cultural conventions shows gratitude and improves the quality of the encounter.

- Convey Your Thanks for the Culture:

Demonstrate an interest in and admiration for Portuguese language, food, music, and history. When tourists show an interest in the customs of the locals, they are often happy.

In Lisbon, friendliness, openness, and a desire to connect allow people to communicate despite linguistic obstacles. By adopting these language and communication strategies, you'll not only make exchanges go more smoothly but also enhance your trip, enabling you to make deep connections and enduring memories in this fascinating city.

Safety and etiquettes

Taking care of business and following customs are two of the most important things a visitor can do in Lisbon. Lisbon, a city well-known for its lively culture and kind hospitality, provides tourists with a secure environment. Like any big city, however, knowing a few safety precautions and cultural customs may make a big difference in how enjoyable and beneficial your visit is. Here are some excellent pointers for Lisbon safety and manners:

- Safety Tips:

1. Safeguard Your Property:

Like any big tourist site, Lisbon is typically secure, although there is always a chance of petty theft. Make sure your possessions are secure by keeping a watch on them, particularly in busy places, on public transit, and at tourist attractions. Put pricey things in anti-theft bags or pouches and refrain from flashing them.

2. Exercise Caution in Tourist Areas:

Tourist-heavy locations should be avoided since pickpockets may target them. Keep a careful eye on your possessions, especially in crowded areas like trams, marketplaces, and well-known sites.

3. Make Use of Licensed Vehicles:

Choose authorized and reliable companies while utilizing ride-sharing or taxis. To prevent any disagreements, make sure the taxi meter is functioning or decide on a fee in advance.

4. Adhere to Local Laws:

Become familiar with the rules and legislation that apply in your area. For instance, there may be penalties for smoking in forbidden locations or consuming alcohol in public. Pay attention to and abide by the city's regulations.

5. Health Services and Emergency Contacts:

Have emergency numbers on hand, such as the 112 number for the local police and the hospital providers. Lisbon has first-rate medical services, but in case of emergency, having travel insurance may provide you extra piece of mind.

- Etiquette Tips:

1. Salutations and Etiquette:

Courtesies and deference are highly regarded in Portuguese culture. Depending on the time of day, greet someone with "Bom dia" (good morning), "Boa tarde" (good afternoon), or "Boa noite" (good evening/night). To be polite, say "Por favor" (please) and "Obrigado/a" (thank you).

2. Modesty and Clothing Code:

Lisbon has permissive dress regulations, yet it's polite to wear modest clothing when you visit places of worship or fancy dining establishments. In such areas, try to avoid wearing clothes that is too exposing to respect local norms.

3. Methods of Tipping:

In Lisbon, leaving a tip is customary but not required. If the service fee is not included, it is typical to tip the server 5–10% of the total bill in restaurants. Tipping taxi drivers and hotel personnel is also customarily appreciated.

4. Manners for Mealtime:

When dining, wait to eat until the host or other guests have finished. Taste the food from the area and honor eating customs. Unless it's conventional for the particular cuisine, use utensils instead of your hands while eating.

5. Honor Cultural Areas:

Be polite when you visit places of worship or historical sites. Stay away from loud discussions, abide by the restrictions regarding photography, and obey any further instructions posted at these locations.

6. Language Consideration::

Even though English is the primary language in Lisbon, trying to speak a few simple Portuguese words demonstrates your appreciation for the local way of life. When tourists attempt to converse in their language, the locals often find it admirable.

Lisbon extends a warm welcome to tourists, and the experience is made better by adhering to local traditions and safety precautions. Travelers may fully immerse themselves in the rich legacy of the city, establish unique encounters, and explore this alluring location by adhering to these safety precautions and cultural etiquette.

Useful apps and resources

With so many helpful applications and tools at your disposal, seeing a bustling city like

Lisbon is immensely simpler and more fulfilling in the digital age. Many applications and websites cover every facet of your Lisbon experience, whether you're looking to discover the finest restaurants, take use of public transit, visit the city's cultural attractions, or learn more about local events. This is a fantastic list of tools and applications that you should not miss when visiting Lisbon:

1. Citymapper and Google Maps:

Google Maps is still a reliable navigational aid in Lisbon and other parts of the globe. Google Maps provides thorough maps and instructions for everything from using public transit to exploring walking paths. Another great tool for navigating urban transportation is Citymapper, which offers up-to-date information on buses, metro, trams, and ferries in Lisbon.

2. Open the Official Lisbon App:

A thorough guide to the city, the Visit Lisbon Official App from Turismo de Lisboa includes details on sights, events, dining options, lodging, and public transit. It's a one-stop shop for exploring Lisbon's greatest spots, with offline maps and helpful travel advice.

3. TheFork and Zomato:

Zomato and TheFork are great places to start culinary experiences. Zomato makes it simpler to find local restaurants by providing menus, reviews, ratings, and images of restaurants located across Lisbon. Users of TheFork may browse restaurants and book tables while often receiving special offers and discounts.

4. Lisboa Card App

The official Lisboa Card app offers information on attractions, deals, and public transit access if you have acquired the Lisboa Card. It's a useful tool for organizing your schedule and making the most of your Lisboa Card while you're here.

5. Bolt and Uber:

Popular ride-sharing applications in Lisbon that provide dependable and practical transit choices include Uber and Bolt. These applications provide a convenient and affordable way to go about the city as an alternative to public transportation and taxis.

6. Portugal's Comboios:

The CP - Comboios de Portugal app provides information on train timetables, itineraries, and ticket sales for trips to neighboring cities and areas for those who want to go outside of Lisbon. It's especially helpful if you want to go outside of Lisbon.

7. Lisbon Culture Agenda:

Use the Culture Agenda Lisboa app to stay up to date on exhibits, concerts, festivals, and other cultural events taking place in Lisbon. It gives you access to a full schedule of cultural events so you can fully experience the thriving arts community in the city.

8. EMEL and ParkMe:

The ParkMe and EMEL (Empresa Municipal de Mobilidade e Estacionamento de Lisboa) applications help you locate parking spots while driving across the city and provide details on parking zones, costs, and availability.

9. Duolingo and the Portuguese Phrasebook:

Apps such as Portuguese Phrasebook and Duolingo are useful for language acquisition and practice of fundamental Portuguese phrases. Even though Portuguese is the primary language in Lisbon, learning a few words in the language can improve your interactions and experiences.

10. Viva Viagem (Lisbon Public Transport Cards):

If you want to easily utilize Lisbon's public transportation system, think about utilizing the Viva Viagem card. Single-trip tickets and other pass options for buses, trams, metro, and trains may be loaded into the card.

These applications and services cover a range of Lisbon experiences, from food and transportation to language support and cultural discovery. Making use of these resources will expedite your journey, improve your comprehension of the city, and guarantee a more pleasurable and knowledgeable stay in Lisbon.

CONCLUSION

We are honored that you have decided to travel with our Lisbon travel guide as you discover one of the most fascinating cities in all of Europe. We've tried to provide a thorough introduction to Lisbon on these pages, highlighting its fascinating history, lively culture, and undiscovered gems.

This handbook aims to be your go-to reference for exploring Lisbon's quaint districts, finding its famous sites, and savoring its delectable cuisine—from the ancient Alfama area to the breathtaking vistas along the Tagus River.

Essential topics including lodging choices, travel advice, language and manners recommendations, safety precautions, and suggested applications and services have all been addressed in order to make your time in Lisbon even more enjoyable.

Our aim has been to provide you with the information and resources need to maximize your visit, guaranteeing a delightful and unforgettable stay in this beautiful city.

May this book be your reliable travel companion, assisting you as you navigate the cobblestone streets, extending an invitation to sample the regional cuisine, and inspiring you to fully immerse yourself in the rich cultural diversity that makes Lisbon such a unique travel destination.

As you discover Lisbon's marvels, I'm wishing you treasured memories and moments that will never be forgotten. I hope your trip through this energetic city is full of happiness, exploration, and treasured experiences. Safe travels.

Printed in Great Britain
by Amazon

37901474R00096